AF326545

The Way to Wisdom

A Leader's Weekly Guide

Teresa G. Carey, Executive Coach

ISBN 978-0-9972756-6-7 (hardcover)

PREFACE

I'm the Founder and Owner of the boutique coaching firm, PerformancePointe, Inc., where performance and excellence have continued to meet for 30 years. What's been discovered deserves to live on.

In anticipation of my 30-year milestone in business as a talent development professional, I've dug deeply over the past several months to unearth some of my most treasured pearls of wisdom. These are not Google-searched or AI-generated—they didn't need to be. This collection was born from three decades of sweat equity and being in the trenches with some of the world's best and brightest leaders.

As an executive and leadership coach, I've evangelized engaging in think time and journaling for as long as I can remember. It's become increasingly evident that the way an individual conceptualizes and processes information determines how freely their thoughts flow in journaling. One of the questions that most commonly surfaces is, "When you ask me to journal, what should I write?" This has taught me that many leaders crave more structure in their journaling practice.

In my own think time, an idea pursued me: *What if I had a worthwhile and rewarding way to share many of the leadership lessons from my work as a coach over three decades?* However, lessons alone weren't powerful enough for facilitating forward thinking and change. It became acutely clear that the lessons needed richer context. The result is this journal.

It is my fervent belief that the truths contained in these pages are both sage and ageless—they stand the test of time. Regardless of what other dynamic, challenging forces are happening around us, these ideas are a closely held compass that can be counted on in any circumstance.

As an adjective, the word "sage" means "wise," or "having

good judgment." As a noun, in classical philosophy, a sage was a person who had attained wisdom and who was seen as virtuous. With intention, we can all become more discerning and wiser through a collection of experiences over time. Reflection and repeated application of the lessons from our experiences develop wisdom as an earned and trusted companion.

Lessons without reflection are merely knowledge. We forfeit the depth of understanding available from our experiences if we don't sit in what our reflective moments can teach us about the people and situations we encounter.

In coaching pre-rapid-growth and rapid-growth executives and leaders, there are countless changes daily both personally and organizationally. It's comforting to know there are some things that are immutable. We all need a strong reference point— a North Star and a guidepost to help us on our journey.

My hope is that you will find this to be a treasured toolkit that will serve and shepherd you not just in the coming weeks and year, but also in the many seasons of leadership to come.

INTRODUCTION

Giving a nod to the meaning of our company name, "pointe," as a place, while also making a learning point, this journal is formatted in weekly segments captioned as "Pointes of Wisdom." Companion coaching questions accompany these as "Reflection Pointes." Together, they are designed to stir deeper thought and application for each weekly experience. This process guides you to and through the weekly way to wisdom.

To glean the most from your way to wisdom experience, work through each journaling prompt each week of the year. You can start at any time, in any week, and carry it through for a full year or longer. Some prompts might require more contemplation. Give yourself space for what it takes to optimize your learning around each journaling discovery. You may find yourself compelled to sit on a single Pointe of Wisdom for more than one week.

After 13 weeks of processing through each week, there is a quarterly reflection designed to capture your learning moments. This segment emphasizes how to share and perpetuate the wisdom you've earned within yourself, your team, and organization. At the end of 52 weeks, there is a one-year review. It will challenge you to summarize the most meaningful Pointes of Wisdom collected, and how you will pull those forward into the future to be a wiser and stronger leader.

Some common themes are intentionally carried through more than one quarter to deepen the wisdom. Although the journal is formatted in consecutive weeks numerically, feel free to skip around if another Pointe of Wisdom feels more applicable.

During your think time or deep work, reflect on the prompt and coaching questions for that week. What fortuitously finds you and captures your attention? How can you step into each sage moment to be a better leader or a more insightful person?

What matters most is that you engage in journaling and

reflection on a consistent basis. The healthy habits we immerse ourselves in regularly form the foundation for who we become.

Birthed from the teachers of time and experience, these lessons and application challenges then translate into your personal and professional journey as you seek and earn sage wisdom. This immeasurable gift will live within you and manifest itself for years to come.

Knowledge is learned. Wisdom is earned.

Dedicated to My Clients as well as
Those Who Have Guided Me Along My Journey

Weekly Pointe of Wisdom

If you're not journaling, you may be forfeiting a winning business idea, a rock star presentation, or the immeasurable growth that comes from reflection.

The practice of journaling got a hold on me about 20 years ago. It's given me every good reason to stay faithful. Writing a pop-up thought or a stream of consciousness idea onto a page is like salve for the soul and hope for the heart. "Why is this thought finding me?" and "What adventure might this take me on?" are always the questions that show up first.

When we take the time to push thoughts onto paper, it:

- Promotes learning by improving memory.
- Allows for meditative thinking, reducing stress.
- Spurs creativity and problem-solving.

Finding a journal with a design that speaks to you allows you to feel drawn to it. Soon it becomes like a companion, at your side. Two easy hacks for beginning to embrace journaling are:

- Dictate notes to your phone, so that, when your journal isn't nearby, you don't lose the brilliant thought.

- Always have a notepad nearby. When you're on the phone, in a virtual meeting, or in another setting not conducive to journaling, the idea or thought stays alive, ready to be transferred into the journal later.

Reflection Pointes

If you're not journaling currently, what are your pre-conceived thoughts about this practice that stand in the way?*

Based on any of the variables happening in your current role or situation, what do you see as the key benefit to you in taking the time to write down your thoughts in a journal?

If you knew that channeling the thoughts from your brain into writing would lead to increasing your effectiveness, how would that motivate you? What are some other motivators?

Who are the people within your sphere who journal? How would you describe them? How does this inspire you to start journaling?

*Congratulations! By engaging in this first Pointe of Wisdom, you're on your way to journaling!

Weekly Pointe of Wisdom
*Never underestimate the importance
of over-communication.*

We say it once and we think it's locked in. The reality is that we've processed this message inside of our heads repeatedly without saying it. Or, within a small circle, perhaps you've socialized it once or twice. Do you want your communication sticky, remembered, and bought into?

For broader-scale strategic communication, say it at least seven times in different ways — verbally in meetings, in writing in emails and newsletters, and through others who are influential in your organization and can help you carry the message forward. Always check for understanding to make sure those around you have it dialed in precisely. Asking what was understood by your message is not overkill.

On a smaller scale, when a leader shares that a team member or a team isn't meeting milestones or deadlines, I always take them back to how it was communicated. Usually, it was only one time, in a meeting, without any follow-up written communication. This is a recipe for missed expectations and disappointment.

Remember, the noise and distraction we are all dealing with in work and life on a daily basis might be crowding out the one thing that you want others to remember most. If you need something captured and acted upon, rinse and repeat it often.

Reflection Pointes

What message are you currently formulating that you need to create a communication plan around?

What are your different methods of communicating it?

Who are your ambassadors who can help you champion the message?

What is the story or narrative you'll share that will make the message most compelling?

Weekly Pointe of Wisdom

When you're not sure, just ask. It's easier
than burning energy trying to interpret it.

What a simple concept. Many coaching conversations are allocated to what approach should be taken to interpret another's comments or actions. There's often fear attached to leaning into the discomfort of asking for clarity. Usually, the person doesn't want to appear unsure in front of another leader, or there might be a concern that approaching it in the moment may stir up conflict.

How much time and energy would you be able to save and reallocate to other, more important activities by simply asking questions? Slow down. Ask these three conversation starters:

- "Can you help me understand this more? I think I'm missing part of the needed information."

- "What's your goal in X situation? Having more insight will allow me to collaborate with you in a more effective way."

- "This is such an important topic/project — can you walk through it again with me? I have a few questions."

Einstein said it best: "A prudent question is one-half of wisdom. One who never asks either knows everything or nothing."

Reflection Pointes

What's a situation you're currently in that requires greater curiosity and clarity?

What's the one thing you're most afraid of facing in this situation?

How can curiosity become the antidote to your fear?

What questions can you ask that will provide the clarity you're seeking?

Weekly Pointe of Wisdom

*A great leader doesn't mind who gets the credit.
An extraordinary leader will always make
sure someone else does.*

When a leader says, "That was my idea, but no one is giving me credit," it usually means there's either some extra ego at play or a deficit of appreciation in another area. A rite of passage in leadership is a new, transformed awareness, mindset, and set of behaviors that gives credit to others over self. A leader of words and action — not just *title* — makes it about the win for the team and organization, regardless of whose idea or project it was.

If you think about post-game interviews of the greatest leaders and coaches, they invariably shine the spotlight on team members and divert the credit to others. As the saying goes, "There's no 'I' in the word 'team.'" Think of the best leaders you know. They don't have an issue with who gets the credit; they are focused on the greater good of the team and the overall strategy.

Once this shift occurs, leadership becomes more satisfying. Team members feel more rewarded and engaged. Everyone wins.

Reflection Pointes

Think of a recent time when you spearheaded a project and took the credit. In hindsight, how would you have managed highlighting others' contributions more than your own, given this week's Pointe of Wisdom?

How does taking the credit — accidentally or purposefully — diminish others on your team in a way that may compromise engagement and retention?

How does the multiplier effect* suggest that allowing others to share in or take the credit will pay off in both the short and long run?

If you remove yourself from the spotlight and give credit to others instead, what will you gain? What will you lose?

*The "multiplier effect" creates positive exponential impact from the leadership approach used in developing a team member.

Weekly Pointe of Wisdom

*Sit in silence regularly. You'll be surprised
at what you hear.*

How often do you allow yourself to just sit — no phone, no
computer, no TV — giving yourself permission to just be? In
today's social media circles, there is a common saying: "Busyness
does not equal productivity" or "Saying you're busy isn't a
badge of honor." Yet, we continue to be caught in the proverbial
vortex of "doing" vs. "being."

Have we sacrificed the life-changing benefits of silence on the
altar of outcomes and achievement?

Whether you're an introvert or an extrovert, in the interest of
strategic thinking, quietness is craved. The tug of life and work
can hijack our intention and execution of seeking "think time." It
takes discipline and focus to stay centered in silence. To enforce
the importance of honoring stillness, start these actions:

- Block dedicated time on the calendar.

- Let others know, so that they can reinforce accountability.

- Ask others on your team to adopt this practice at least weekly
  for their own wellness and productivity.

Reflection Pointes

- Where is the best "sit spot" — away from your normal workspace — that allows you to sit and think?

- Knowing your own daily or weekly flow of energy, what's your optimal time for thinking? For many, the morning hours allow for the greatest clarity.

- How can you best protect your silence and think time? If you place a block on your schedule as "CEO time," how likely are you to keep the appointment with yourself, your own CEO? What other options might work?

- Practice think time for three weeks/21 days. What happens to your energy? Your clarity? Your creativity?

Weekly Pointe of Wisdom
Time is the only finite resource.
Steward it wisely.

You're in charge of your time when you understand that saying "No" can make the difference between excellence and mediocrity in the areas that matter most. It can be the differentiator in quality of life, stress management, and overall well-being. Knowing what's most important can drive our priorities or non-negotiables, making it much easier for us to say "No" or "Yes" to any given request.

Those who practice weekly planning time are most effective. Writing down the three most imperative priorities each day allows greater focus and intention. Tying the priorities to weekly, monthly, and annual goals tethered to the firm's strategy ensures alignment. By knowing what success looks like within this framework, it's much more likely time will be stewarded with the care it deserves.

Benjamin Franklin said it best: "Dost thou love life? Then do not squander time, for that is the stuff that life is made of."

Reflection Pointes

What are the one to three most important things in your life?

As you look at your schedule, what percentage of your time is allocated to each of these areas?

How does importance stand up against the time allocated? What adjustments can you start making today?

If you said "No" to something, what would it be? Create a "Do Not Do" list. What happens to your use of time and overall productivity?

Weekly Pointe of Wisdom
*Values-based thinking allows decisions
to flow much more easily.*

Decision-making, especially in high-stakes situations, can be one of the hardest things you do as a leader and a professional. How do you know what's best? Is there a right and wrong answer in any given situation? If you know your values and honor them, invariably, you will make the decision that honors who you are and what's called for in that defining moment. The guesswork is gone.

What's most important to you? What practices do you regularly engage in? Where do you put your time? What do you believe so fervently in that you're willing to debate or fight for it? Often these are clues to our values.

The purpose-filled leaders I know have defined their values and use them as a guiding force for all aspects of their life and business. It's made all the difference. When you're a values-based leader, you increase respect for yourself and from others. Your mind and heart are free from overthinking in all situations. Clarity catapults.

Reflection Pointes

If you need a frame of reference, there are multiple values lists available online. If you narrow these down to five to seven personal values, what values are represented on your list?

As you are zeroing in on your values, ask those who know you best what values they consistently see in you and your behaviors. What patterns emerge?

What decision/s are you currently making that you can hold up against your values? Ask yourself, "What would someone with my values do?" How does this make any decision/s easier?

What time and energy are saved because your values serve as the compass that increases certainty about the direction you should go?

Weekly Pointe of Wisdom

*No one wants you to succeed at a presentation
more than your listeners.*

It's often said that we are more afraid of giving presentations than we are of dying. That's a staggering thought. Where are you on the spectrum of anxiety and fear when it comes to delivering a presentation?

When you're seeking to share a powerful presentation, use these three pointers:

1. Visualize yourself as the doctor who is delivering a healing message to the minds of the people who have come to hear it.

2. Stop and realize that *you're* the one in the room who knows the most about your topic. *You* are the expert. Present in the way *you* want others to see *you* and *your* expertise.

3. Prepare to achieve the desired outcome. Organize your message into one key theme and three supporting points. Rehearse three to five times in order to hit your stride when you're ready to deliver. Video yourself presenting. The camera doesn't lie. What does it show and teach you?

Reflection Pointes

Think of an upcoming presentation. What's your number-one concern or fear?

How have you overcome this in the past? How can you leverage this same technique now? When you organize and prepare based on Technique Number 3 , how does it boost your confidence and allay your fears?

Visualize yourself in the room in front of the group. Picture yourself presenting comfortably and effortlessly. See the audience nodding, listening intently, and smiling. This is what connection looks like.

With the recommended physical and mental preparation tips, anticipate and soak in the desired response. Journal post-presentation what you did to create this outcome and how you can continue to raise your personal bar.

Weekly Pointe of Wisdom
*Just because you can,
it doesn't mean you should.*

In an entrepreneurial or rapid-growth culture, optimism runs rampant out of necessity. There's often a rush to be first to market or to make a sweeping new change. Taking on too much too soon, or getting side-tracked in a secondary area of focus, can take down the house.

Heroism sometimes holds founders and leaders captive in pursuing the next bold move. *Shiny Object Syndrome* has sent many leaders down a trail of distraction and subsequent opportunity cost. The lure of what's possible is powerful. That's not necessarily bad, unless it detracts from keeping the main thing, the main thing.

It's often best to take a hard look at choosing the next thing wisely. Traction can set the tempo when tempered behavior helps to set the tone. Staying centered on what's most imperative requires discipline and deliberate patience with a well-thought-out plan that's already in place. Unless there's a market disruption demanding a different direction, stay purposed and "on Pointe."

Reflection Pointes

What's a current opportunity or initiative you're considering? How does it fit within or support the blueprint already in place?

How does it potentially detract from the focus on the bigger plan? What are you willing to trade off?

If you followed the rule, "If it's a good option today, it will still be a good option tomorrow," what action would you take? In thinking longer term, will the value it presents today be available in the future?

What disciplines can you adopt to keep you focused on the main thing?

Weekly Pointe of Wisdom

*The moment you realize you're paid to **think** more than **do**, your leadership quotient multiplies.*

There's a turning point in every leader's journey. If you're an entrepreneurial leader, you're often wearing multiple hats until you can hire those who are better and smarter than you for each operational function. Letting go of control can be one of the hardest steps to take along the path to scale.

What's the irony? By letting go of doing, you gain *even more control and power*. You are free from being controlled by responsibilities others can manage, allowing for your focus to be on the more strategic and broader scope that's imperative for the path ahead.

The realization of being paid to think is about shifting what you value and enjoy from your role, to driving the most value for the entire organization. Increasingly, the scope should shift to vision-caster, strategist, communicator, resource-giver, and developer.

Reflection Pointes

Currently, what are the most valuable and enjoyable parts of your role? Which of these are more functional, as opposed to strategic? If you started by letting just one of these go and finding a different option for getting it done, which part would it be?

Would you pay someone the same compensation that you receive for doing all the things you're currently doing? What doesn't align with your level?

What can you do with the time saved that would better serve your organization?

As you're growing your team and organization, continue to re-evaluate your role and the parts that can be delegated or eliminated. Notice how this opens the space for more strategic, valuable *thinking* as opposed to *doing*. What happens?

Weekly Pointe of Wisdom
*Never apologize for choosing your
faith, family, or fitness first.*

We are faced multiple times daily with the need to evaluate priorities and honor boundaries. If you went through the values activity outline in week seven, then your values should give you permission to honor what's most important. The leaders I know constantly struggle with balancing personal priorities with professional demands. What does balance look like for you?

The balance of time begins with a declaration of *First Things First.** To determine this, look inward. Noticing what creates the most happiness and energy can provide strong clues. In addition, look to the future, and consider what would constitute a life well-lived. Allow for connecting daily time practices to that vision.

The National Institute of Health researched the five most common regrets of those who were dying. Their "I wish" list included:

1. I wish I'd had the courage to live a life true to myself, not the life others expected of me.

2. I wish I hadn't worked so hard.

3. I wish I'd had the courage to express my feelings.

4. I wish I'd stayed in touch with my friends.

5. I wish I'd let myself be happier.

Reflection Pointes

Look at your calendar and bank statement. What's the reality of where your time and money are going? This is a strong indication of your current priorities.

Based on this assessment, what time allocation in an average week of 720 hours would you aspire to give to:

- Family
- Faith
- Fitness/Wellness
- Fun
- Financial/Work

What time robbers most interfere with your ability to create space for what matters most? For many leaders, it's social media or the demands of others — coffee or networking meetings, over-dependence of a team member, or any number of other requests.

*Stephen Covey, The Seven Habits of Highly Effective People.

Weekly Pointe of Wisdom
*Resonance or dissonance tells you everything
you need to know about certainty.*

The investment of reflection touted in this work yields the return of self-awareness. It allows us to get in touch with and become intimately familiar with how we feel about the world around us and our own inner truth.

How does resonance apply? When we're listening, really listening, to our minds, heart, and gut, they give off signals that inform us. Resonance yields peace and calm. Conversely, dissonance tells us when something is off. When we are around others or faced with a situation that isn't right for us, we have limbic or cognitive dissonance. The feeling is off, we're in a fog, or our energy is drained, causing us to manifest physical symptoms as one signal.

When faced with your next scenario you're not sure how to approach or handle, let your feelings of resonance or dissonance inform your typical logic-based approach. It will tell you everything you should know for the certainty you're seeking.

Reflection Pointes

What clarity or certainty are you currently seeking?

As you consider the next step or ultimate outcome, what are you feeling? Inner peace, turmoil, slight unrest, happiness, other? Then, label the emotion — is it fear, excitement, anxiety, frustration, or anticipation…? Journal what you are experiencing. What does this tell you?

Think back to a time when you were faced with a similar situation or decision. When you had a positive outcome, what feelings led you to make that specific choice?

When you had an undesirable outcome, how were your feelings informing you? Did you have the "knowingness" to be able to process them and realize what was happening? How can you allow a different outcome today, based on what you know now?

Weekly Pointe of Wisdom

Everyone has been hurt or is hurting.
Grace and kindness are a healing balm.
Apply liberally.

My daughter recently asked me if I thought the pain I had experienced during a certain season of my life better equipped me for understanding and abiding with others who are hurting or facing challenges. There wasn't an immediate answer — only a deserved pause. The answer finally emerged: "Well, I believe the more trouble or pain we've faced, the greater our empathy and ability to extend grace."

It's often easy to criticize those who didn't show up the way we expect. While there are standards to be met, understanding and kindness should accompany the expectation.

Someone once said, "Grace is the face that love wears when it meets imperfection." How are you dealing with imperfections in the world around you — with frustration, anger, or impatience? Or are you able to embrace an imperfection with love?

Reflection Pointes

Look in the mirror. Think of a time in your professional and personal life when you fell short of expectations. Who was there to reassure and inspire you to move forward? What difference did this make in your growth and your ability to advance?

If you judged yourself with the same standard with which you judge others, what would that look like?

Who in your current team or organization needs an additional dose of kindness and understanding? Without over-compromising performance metrics or values, what do you want to start doing differently today in the way you individually navigate this situation?

If a conversation about an employee's performance is necessary, outline the points you would make that demonstrate greater understanding and empathy. What are your talking points?

Quarterly
Wisdom Reflection Pointes

What one applied Pointe from the journal has been most meaningfu
for you during the past quarter?

How has this made you a better leader or person?

What is the story or narrative you can share about this shift
with others, so that the impact continues within your team and
organization? A potential story outline might look like the following

- "Here was the situation…"

- "Here's what prompted me to work on it…"

- "Here are the actions I took that mattered…"

- "The positive outcome/s include…"

- "How might a similar approach help you in any of your
  current situations?"

Additional Reflection Pointes

Weekly Pointe of Wisdom
If you view conflict as merely a disagreement or an information gap, it's much easier to lean into and resolve.

Our adeptness at managing a conflict is often tied to our leadership profile and the system in which we operate. Any or all of these conditions affect how we perceive and navigate conflict.

- **Personal Perception** — Those who view conflict as an argument, a fight, or a confrontation are less eager to engage in conversations that elicit differing points of view. Those who feel communication is necessary to expose and resolve divergent opinions move into conflict more easily. It's a *conversation*, and the outcome will be either that we agree or that we agree to disagree. That's it.

- **Hard-wiring of Strengths** — The Gallup organization, creators of the world-renowned StrengthsFinder™, find those who are lower in a Strength like Harmony — or, conversely, higher in a Strength like Command — are more comfortable with disagreement.

- **Organizational Culture** — Some cultures embrace conflict, while others delay discussing it and may even avoid it altogether. Consequently, passive-aggressive behaviors might become the norm by keeping those who disagree with us out of the loop. The more there's encouragement to work through disagreement, the safer everyone feels about offering up and pushing through areas of conflict.

Conflict is merely a harder-than-normal conversation. And if it ends with agreeing to disagree, that may be the greatest win.

Reflection Pointes

What's your defining narrative for conflict? What has shaped how you view and manage conflict?

What conversation do you need to have that will clear the air and reduce the amount of emotional energy you're investing in thinking about it?

If your view is out of alignment with what you want it to be, how can you start to view it as, "It's simply a conversation, and the outcome will be either that we agree or that we agree to disagree"?

How can you make disagreement conversations safer within your team and organization? What actions can you take to normalize conflict? Model it? State the expectation? Declare values that encourage it? Other?

Weekly Pointe of Wisdom

As a leader, if you hang on to the project or thing you love but should let go, you're forfeiting someone else's opportunity to stretch and grow.

We've likely all heard the overused phrase "Delegate to elevate." It sounds easy enough. The reality is that *we all love doing what we love to do.* However, if we're going to shift from being a functional leader to an enterprise-wide leader — or even just grow beyond our current state to the next level — we have to delegate.

As we adopt the mindset of a servant leader, we realize we're robbing someone else of the opportunity to become stronger and better, simply by not letting go.

What are you holding onto that is holding you and someone else back from what should be the natural progression of growth? You have to know what it is before you can calculate the opportunity cost. If a tree doesn't lose its leaves in the fall, it doesn't come back bigger and stronger in the spring. Shedding and letting go should be continual practices for ourselves and those around us if we want to collectively evolve to the next level.

Reflection Pointes

Make a list of your main responsibilities and projects that dominate your time. Which ones can be delegated, based on the aspiration of where you are as a leader and where you and your team or firm are headed within the next year?

Review your high-potential (HiPo=those who are high performers and have potential) list. Who should these responsibilities be delegated to as stretch opportunities?

As you delegate these, determine a better and higher use of your own time.

Where will this same time be allocated? Engaging in more deep work and think time, forming and nurturing strategic relationships, and developing others are all imperative next-level time optimizers.
w

Weekly Pointe of Wisdom
*What you need will always find you
if you leave space for it.*

Fifteen years ago, I reached a turning point in how I viewed overinvesting in situations or people who didn't align with my values, or what I wanted to attract as part of my life and future. One of my friends drew my attention to an article on just-in-time thinking. The premise with this mindset is born of abundance. It spoke to trusting that you'll always have what you need if your actions and beliefs align with what you're seeking.

To get what you need, you may need to make space by ridding yourself of the things that are incongruent with your desires. If you have a person in your life who is toxic or an energy vampire, they are taking a place that could be occupied by a healthy relationship or an energy-giver. Similarly, if you're in a career, volunteer role, or other position that doesn't serve you, you are preventing the right thing from showing up because there's no room.

Notice if you're potentially staying involved because of the time already invested. However, sunk cost is never a reason to stay invested in a lost cause. Move on, knowing that what's ahead is going to be exponentially worth more than what you're giving up. Count on it.

Reflection Pointes

What's the number-one desire of your heart?
Start with the list below. Claim it today.

- Healthier relationships?

- More time freedom?

- A more thriving business?

- Deeper spiritual connection?

- Other?

What are you holding onto that is potentially interfering with
your desire finding you?

If you let one person or thing go that isn't serving you and you've
overextended the investment, what one step do you need to take to
move it out of your life, so that the one thing you most want
can move into that space?

Weekly Pointe of Wisdom

*Don't confuse humility with a lack of confidence.
Leaders who are the most secure have a
healthy dose of both.*

Humility and confidence — it's a juxtaposition that's often misunderstood. Is it possible to strike a balance between these two attributes and their related behaviors? Humility says, "I am who I am, and I'm comfortable with that," and "I'm not above others." Confidence exudes a sense of boldness and self-assurance. These aren't mutually exclusive, thank goodness.

Consider these as opportunities to be confident in your own abilities yet recognize when team members may be stronger in other areas. Humility can say with confidence:

- "I was wrong. Thank you for sharing another perspective."

- "I don't know. I haven't been here before. What would you do?"

- "What am I not considering in this situation?"

The confidence and security to be humble — what a refreshing and respected approach to leading and living!

Reflection Pointes

As you self-assess, how do you believe you demonstrate humility? How about confidence?

Think of a recent time when you were out of balance in either of these behaviors. What happened?

Using this as an example, what typically leads you to overuse or underuse in either area?

Looking at where you are today, what opportunities exist to demonstrate a healthy blend of confidence and humility? How can you incorporate both into your way of being so it becomes a part of your core and who you are as a person and leader?

Weekly Pointe of Wisdom

When you launch a business or start anything new, you won't have all the answers. You have to be comfortable with ambiguity.

In working with thousands of business start-ups, developing leaders and career-changers over the past 30 years, one takeaway is that successful agility is tethered to a high comfort with ambiguity. Some who don't have all the perceived answers become stuck, while others know they'll figure it out along the way. The most important first step is being able to take the first step.

Why do some great ideas never get launched? How does someone with talent hit an artificial ceiling of potential? What causes an appetite for change and learning new skills in some and an aversion or hesitancy to these in others?

The inability to execute is just a symptom of a much deeper issue. The causes of failure to launch, talent ceilings, and learning new things are typically tied to over analysis, a lack of belief in abilities, or not enough practice in change. It might also be tied to the support systems (or a lack of) around the individual. How can you become more comfortable?

- Set shorter milestones and steps in place, as opposed to giant leaps.

- Center on small wins and small failures. It's easier to build traction off incremental wins and easier to recover from failures.

- Follow the 80% rule. If you have 80% of the information, that's your go-forward point.

- Listen to your gut and heart — as outlined in Week 12.

- Have an accountability buddy or two to encourage and inspire you.

Reflection Pointes

What have you been delaying that needs to be acted upon? Start now by writing what the end result or goal looks like.

What's held you back so far? What's the one interference you've faced?

Using any or all of the five tactics offered, how can you take the next step starting today?

Who do you have in your corner you can share the vision with, and who will be a continued sounding board and inspiration for moving forward? What other resources are needed to get traction?

Weekly Pointe of Wisdom

Coaching is simply asking questions that help others to become aware of and act on the areas they aren't able to resolve on their own.

One of the most misunderstood roles of a leader is the role of coach. There is a stereotypical view of having an athletic coach, who was continually in the position of telling us what we were doing well and what we could improve upon. The discipline of workplace coaching is different.

As adults, we learn best from experiences. These experiences allow us, in our own awareness, to solve many of our own dilemmas and create clarity. We just need to be asked the right questions that take us to the answers.

Thinking about coaching as leading, not telling, is one of the best ways to remember our role as a coach — with team members, peers, and other stakeholders. A commonly held belief is that it takes more time to ask questions than it does to just give someone the answer. In reality, it's more efficient.

By asking a few questions, here's what happens:

- It allows for critical reflection and analysis, yielding a better solution.

- It creates deeper buy-in — people believe what *they* say more than what we *tell* them.

- It empowers the person to become more self-correcting and self-generating, reducing future over-reliance on others for help.

Reflection Pointes

- Are you a solution giver or a solution seeker? Depending on your answer, how can you increase your tendency to coach instead of tell in seeking solutions from others?

- How can you begin practicing a more defined coaching approach*? Here are some questions to get you started:

  - "How do you feel project X went?"

  - "What did you do well to help drive the result? Looking back, what would you do differently?"

  - "How might you leverage these lessons in the upcoming project on Y?"

  - "If you had a magic wand, what would happen?"

  - "What are the steps needed to get there? Which one should you take first?"

- Plan your next coaching conversation. What does success look like?

- After practicing the art of asking instead of telling, what starts to happen? What's the response of the people you are coaching? How do they become more empowered and engaged?

*For more information on the discipline of coaching, read THE COACHING HABIT by Michael Bunjay Stanier.

Weekly Pointe of Wisdom

Play at your best and hire the rest.

How do you know if you're playing at your best? Both your performance and your energy will be high. You'll have reinforced wins within the areas that bring you the most joy. You'll go to bed excited about the next day and wake with anticipation of what's to come as soon as your feet hit the floor. It's *that* different.

This is your genius zone. If you're not here today, it's time to reset.

When we're trapped in the dregs of the most undesirable parts of our role, *everyone* pays the price. The resulting unhappiness reverberates throughout our entire ecosystem. It depletes our motivation and puts a ceiling on our potential.

If you focused on the ROI of what's possible by aligning with your strengths, what might happen for you, your team, and your organization?

Reflection Pointes

What are your top-three strengths — the ones that give you the most joy and energy to apply?

What does it feel like to play at your best? What emotions do you experience? How is your energy-level different?

How do you show up as a leader when you're in this place? What do others say about you? How do they react?

What can you do to more consistently be and stay at your best? What roles should you step out of and create for someone else?

Weekly Pointe of Wisdom

*As a leader, if you can allocate 80% of your time
to listening and 20% of your time to talking,
you'll always walk away smarter.*

It's uncanny how the 80/20 rule applies to so many aspects of life and work. The dance of communication is no different. With leadership, it's important to become a student in learning as you interact with all your other leaders and team members.

Often, as leaders, we can feel the self-imposed expectation of being the smartest person in the room. If you're the smartest person in the room, you're either:

- *hiring the wrong people, or,*

- *you're in the wrong room.*

Hold space for others to do most of the talking. You might be surprised at what you hear from and see in them.

Reflection Pointes

What's your current average ratio of talking as opposed to listening in most meetings?

In what ways can you prepare for less information giving and more information seeking in your meetings this week?

Whose voices need to be heard more? How can you make more space for them?

What questions can you prepare that set the table for others to open up more in meetings? Consider starting with open-ended, broad questions like:

- "What's the one strategically most-important item on today's agenda, and why?"

- "What one emotion describes how you're feeling as we begin today's meeting?"

- "What do you feel is your/our one greatest win for this week? How can we leverage this with project or deal X?"

- "If we could only do one thing differently in how we're leading Y, what would it be?"

- "What's the elephant on the table when it comes to Z?"

Weekly Pointe of Wisdom

At the end of the day, all we really want is to be seen, heard, and understood.

It's unarguable that being present — truly present — when we're with others is one of the greatest gifts we can give them. If we go into a meeting or even into a social situation with obvious distraction, it sends the message to others that they're not as important as the other issue diverting our attention.

An unforgettable moment for me was coaching a leader who had multiple other tasks he was managing during a meeting. I paused; then kindly asked, "Is there something more important that deserves your attention than our time together right now?" He stopped and said, "No. It can wait." This was never an issue moving forward.

We'll always have competing priorities and an infinite number of attention grabbers in our near reach. What we won't have is the opportunity to redeem lost moments with others who matter.

Reflection Pointes

What are the most common distractions that stand in your way of fully focusing on others?

How are you currently managing these?

If you started to apply 15-30 minutes of margin time to "clear the decks" before each meeting, what could happen?

What do you want others to remember about you as a leader and how you made them feel? Based on this desire, how can you start to self-actualize this by how you show up?

Weekly Pointe of Wisdom
*You will always be a villain in someone's story.
How you manage it is what matters.*

The mystery of the human spirit constantly creates intrigue. You're walking out your brand and purpose. You're living your values and being true to yourself. Then, with what may be sudden surprise, someone creates a narrative that makes you the bad guy. When others don't take the time to understand you and your actions, it's easier for them to villainize you.

When you discover there's an issue and reach out to them, there's only silence — which is the greatest form of aggression. Or they may continue to communicate, out of necessity or obligation, but it's cold and lacks any true connection. It can be uncomfortable at least and a bit daunting at worst. What should you do? There are options.

1. Walk away completely and **LTSG:** *Let That [Stuff] Go.*

2. Lean into solving the issue and ask, "What's happened to our relationship?" "What do we need to do to mend what's standing in the way of our connection?" Depending on what unfolds, you can either co-create a plan to heal the relationship or decide it's too far gone and *then* LTSG.

The choice made depends on the stakes tied to the relationship and on the Emotional Intelligence of either party to be able to reconcile. Ultimately, we need to decide what's healthiest and what meaning the relationship brings to our overall wellness.

Reflection Pointes

Think of a relationship that's currently distant or strained and in which you've been made the villain.

Out of the two choices described, or any others you might create, how do you want to move forward?

If you decide to *LTSG,* how will you prevent the relationship and situation from stealing energy and bandwidth?

In alignment with other Weekly Pointes of Wisdom, how does any time that's now available from letting this go allow space for new and healthier people and relationships?

Weekly Pointe of Wisdom

When you can isolate and remove the one thing that's standing in the way of the one thing you want most, your path forward emerges.

A couple of years ago, the word *becomingness* emerged within me as a new concept. I define it as "the pause of anticipation between what is no longer and what is not yet." The first step to becoming is to envision what's ahead and see the potential of what's possible. To reach that point, it's imperative to anticipate obstacles. What would prevent you from getting there?

Start here. Name it specifically.

We have three to seven options when faced with any obstacle. The power of choice enables us to favor one or more alternatives that heighten the probability of a solution.

When we're focused on our goal and figure out how to eliminate what's standing in the way, we are unstoppable. Keep moving forward. You may be only one step short of a breakthrough to becoming.

Reflection Pointes

- Personally, or professionally, what's the one thing you want most on the path to "becomingness"?

- What's the number-one obstacle that would stand in the way of this potential outcome?

- Make a list of the three to seven ways this can be managed or removed.

- List your next three actions to build the traction needed to begin.

Weekly Pointe of Wisdom
It's never too late to do something new and big.

My grandmother, at age 71, on her first Ferris wheel ride, nervously stated, "A fool will leave home and do just about anything." As it turns out, she was right. To do something big and bold, we have to be willing to "leave our home base" of comfort and stretch ourselves beyond what's possible.

It's inspiring to think about the act of reinvention and those who "left home" and what they knew; then they took the needed risks to reach success later in life. Here are a few:

- Julia Childs — She became famous as a TV chef in her 50s.

- Morgan Freeman — In his 50s, he debuted by starring in his first major film.

- Colonel Sanders — He franchised KFC in his 60s.

Starting later in life can be a distinct advantage: we have the accumulated experience, knowledge, and wisdom to actually reduce our risks. Any failures up to this stage of life have equipped us to increase the likelihood of success.

Reflection Pointes

If you stay where you are today, what will happen, and where will you be one year from now? How will you feel?

What does leaving the comfort of home look like for you? What's your one greatest fear?

Picture yourself in your aspirational state. What are you seeing? What are you doing? How are you feeling? Write it down here.

What resources and people can you surround yourself with to encourage and support you, as well as keep you accountable? Who is the first person you can share this with?

Weekly Pointe of Wisdom
Keep your circle small and tight.

There are few things more precious than genuine friends. When you have an overabundant number of people you call "friends" or try to engage in too many close relationships, the law of diminishing returns can set in. Real friends deserve an investment of time and emotional energy. Having a super-sized circle can rob us of deep, meaningful, and lasting connectivity.

We've all seen the meme that declares some people are in our lives for a reason, others are in it for a season, and some are in it for life. If you have a larger circle, it's not unreasonable to think that you would increase the chances of having more lifetime friends, while reason-and-season friends fall by the wayside.

That's not necessarily the case. If you find friends with the same values and keep your inner circle smaller, you have more opportunities to create shared experiences, resulting in a mutually satisfying lifetime bond.

Choose Wisely has never been truer, especially when it comes to authentic and lasting relationships.

Reflection Pointes

Who are the five to seven people in your circle you want to stay connected with for life?

If this is difficult, then ask yourself, "Who are the energy givers?" "Who are the energy takers?" "Who in my circle brings balance?"

How often do you find yourself feeling "friendship fatigue" — brought on by trying to maintain too many relationships — or as if you're acting out of a sense of duty?

How can you manage the relationships that use too much energy differently starting now? How about the ones who give back energy?

Quarterly
Wisdom Reflection Pointes

What one applied Pointe from the journal has been most meaningful for you during the past quarter?

How has this made you a better leader or person?

What is the story or narrative you can share about this shift with others, so that the impact continues within your team and organization? A potential story outline might look like the following:

- "Here was the situation…"

- "Here's what prompted me to work on it…"

- "Here are the actions I took that mattered…"

- "The positive outcome/s include…"

- "How might a similar approach help you in any of your current situations?"

Additional Reflection Pointes

Weekly Pointe of Wisdom
Occasionally, people may surprise you, but mostly count on them rising to your highest level of expectation.

I've watched the Pygmalion effect play out repeatedly over the years. It started early, as a Bluebird reader in the first grade. Even as six-year-olds, the supposed secret was out: Bluebirds were the best readers, Redbirds were average readers, and Yellowbirds were trying their best. I often wonder how this initial imprinting played out for many in life.

In the workplace, we unconsciously label associates as blue, red, or yellow. We think we're hiring the best candidate, and, sometimes, there's an early win or a first-time failure or disappointment. At this defining moment, we may prematurely make our determination of that person's potential.

If you are slow to judge and quick to support, it can transform a team member's path to excellence. Focusing on their strengths while holding timely curbside-coaching sessions on their progress, communicates that you believe in their best and brightest abilities.

Reflection Pointes

How would you describe your current approach to onboarding and leading with the highest — yet practical — expectations?

Who on your team do you see as a Bluebird, Redbird, or Yellowbird? Out of the Redbirds and Yellowbirds, who might be a Bluebird in disguise?

Outline your new-and-improved approach in leading this unassuming team member.

How can you begin to expect the best from everyone on your team, with more intentional performance-management methods?

Weekly Pointe of Wisdom

*No one, not even you, can take your worthiness away.
You were born worthy.*

A friend has built her business on helping individuals see their worth. For many, either their upbringing or the upheavals they've experienced in life have taken a toll on their perception of self and feelings of worth. As I've worked with talented leaders, there are signs of insecurity that are often linked to their diminished sense of worthiness and belonging.

In social media, we see occasional posts focusing on *imposter syndrome.* When we feel we don't belong in our role, at our current level of financial success, or even to be at a place of happiness and fulfillment, it all links back to worth. Worth is a spectrum, not a binary state — where you either have it or you don't.

Stay in tune with moments when you or others you lead may exhibit feelings of unworthiness. A few of the signs are struggling to accept compliments or recognition, or a lack of emotional expression — either good or bad. It can show up as self-sabotage through exhibiting behaviors that hold people back from their fullest potential. Procrastinating when there's enough time for completion, not putting in the available effort, and emotionally acting out in a way that distances team members are all self-defeating strategies you may feel personally or see in others.

Reflection Pointes

In which areas do you struggle with worth?

How about others you lead or work with? Who stands out as someone who may exhibit the signs described in the Pointe of Wisdom?

What are some ways you can begin to affirm yourself? Some leaders keep their resume/bio updated to include accomplishments as a reminder of worth. Others keep a "brag file" that includes complimentary notes, positive performance appraisals, and achievements. What methods might work well for you?

How can you guide and coach team members who might struggle with worth to seek out small wins — as something that allows them to believe in themselves — and, more importantly, their inherent worth as a human?

Weekly Pointe of Wisdom

*Business doesn't have to be overly complicated.
Find a market need. Strive for excellence daily.
Do the right thing. You can be successful.*

While facilitating entrepreneurial business-planning programs*
for thousands of aspiring and growth-based entrepreneurs,
one thing was repeatedly evident: It didn't matter how much
financial backing they had or how great their idea was. If the
product or service didn't fill a need in the marketplace, nothing
else mattered. Feasibility fell flat.

Yet proof of concept was only the beginning. Next, the sweat
equity needed to launch and continue improving, learning, and
growing to meet demand was required. Through each growth
stage, there were defining moments when their values and
integrity were tested. Sometimes doing the right thing meant
losing a customer or stakeholder. Often, it would allow for
attracting and earning those who aligned fortuitously.

Success is defined differently, depending on personal definition.
Some entrepreneurs build a lifestyle business that they control
along each stage of growth (not to be confused with a hobby).
Others strive for a wealth-building venture they can grow, and
then sell or pass down. Regardless of how success is measured
by the founder and other leaders, there are clear steps to viability.
Without oversimplifying the equation, these three steps have
held true in my own business and in others I've been a part of:
*Find a need, perform consistently with excellence, and do the
right thing.*

Reflection Pointes

What are the ways in which you find yourself overcomplicating your business or leadership role?

How can you show up more intrapreneurial or entrepreneurial in thinking like an owner?

If you are the owner, how can you empower others by keeping the vision and mission simple, as outlined above?

What new messaging do you need to create, and what actions do you need to take, to make sure that all of your associates and teams are on the same page with regard to the basics in achieving success?

This week's Pointe of Wisdom is dedicated to the late Ewing Marion Kauffman, entrepreneur, philanthropist, and the Founder of the FastTrac™ experience, where I was a coach and master facilitator for fifteen years.

Weekly Pointe of Wisdom

*Take any potential worry about the competition
and apply it to being your best.*

One of the leaders I coach shared an inspirational card with me after a meaningful meeting. The caption on the card will stay with me forever. It read, "When you stay in your lane, there's no competition." This is an axiom we can all hold on to.

Admittedly, we shouldn't work in a vacuum, ignoring the competitive landscape altogether. However, when we give too much energy to consider what others in our field either are or aren't doing, we waste valuable bandwidth that can be applied to our:

- Creativity

- Problem-solving

- Continued Professional Development

- Focus on Serving Our Customer's Needs

Being at our personal best means operating in our genius zone or sweet spot in a way no one else can. It's the space that uniquely defines and creates a micro-niche for our brand as a leader or business. No one else can show up in our lane, when we're occupying the lane that only we can fill. Play from your strengths, and let others play from theirs, because they are *never* the same.

Reflection Pointes

On a scale of 1-10 (with 1 being "I never give it a thought" and 10 being "It keeps me up at night"), how often are you occupied with thinking about your competition?

If you scored 6 or higher, what can you do with that unproductive preoccupation and re-channel it into focusing on your customers? What do they most want and need?

What one thing do you need to start doing to deliver this in a way that creates unique value and unparalleled value?

If you invested in one new creative, professional development (e.g., certification or training) or a business development initiative designed to impact your own or your business's growth, what would it be?

Weekly Pointe of Wisdom
Values and character are not coachable.

As facilitators of change we often convince ourselves that, with just the right amount of effort and the exact approach, we can improve or even transform others. If we are working to impact competencies, the right development effort can shift someone's thinking, as well as their behavior.

However, two things that are not changeable through coaching are character and the accompanying values (or lack of) that affect a character deficit. The misalignment of either of these leads to frustration, disappointment, and ultimately a severance of the relationship. If we hire or partner with people of character, we save tremendous amounts of emotional burn and bandwidth.

When you hire talent *and* common values combined with character, assimilation into the role and organization are exponentially easier. To unlock the answer to congruence in these two areas, do this:

- Hire based on referrals. Pay for referrals. Great people know great people.

- Create an interviewing process that includes an emphasis on ethics, values, and the behaviors the candidate has demonstrated.

- Ask multiple questions about former situations in which these were tested. Lean into asking the candidate about how they would handle a common challenge within your organization. What do they tell you?

Reflection Pointes

How are you currently assessing character and values in the hiring process?

When there's a character line crossed or values expectation that's violated within your team, how do you currently handle it?

What feedback do you receive on how you manage this area?

What do you want to commit to doing differently to ensure that character and values are elevated as non-negotiables within your hiring approach, performance management process, and overall cultural norms?

Weekly Pointe of Wisdom
Leading with levity is not over-rated.

Bringing appropriate humor can transform how your team experiences every aspect of their work. When fun is fostered either organically or purposefully, perspectives can dramatically and positively shift.

In a recent strategy meeting, the team members selected "fun" as one of their rules of engagement. The CEO and COO offered a few quips and jokes throughout the day, leading the way for others to be playful as well. It significantly lightened the mood, yet still allowed the group to focus and arrive at the intended outcome. Without question, teams who can laugh together experience:

- More cohesion.

- Heightened engagement.

- Greater creativity.

If you want a team and organizational culture that reflects these attributes, then bring occasional levity and laughter into how you lead. It might just be the shortest path to unleashing your organization's next big idea.

Reflection Pointes

How much humor and fun are currently part of your leadership brand or style? Choose one of the following:

- I always use a *taking care of business* approach. We have serious work to do around here!

- I take my cues from others and adjust accordingly.

- Having fun is a core component of our culture and meeting atmosphere.

If you see a potential need for more levity and laughter, what are some ways you can start to model it while not radically departing from who you naturally are?

Think of an upcoming meeting, is there an icebreaker or another activity you can use to add an element of fun?

To give team members permission to use more levity, what are some broader cultural approaches you can leverage to incorporate more playfulness, while not disrupting their focus?

Weekly Pointe of Wisdom
*What you tolerate is what you teach to
be acceptable within your culture.*

How easy or difficult is it for you to overlook certain
unacceptable behaviors, depending on the performance of
the individual? High performers who exhibit culturally
incongruent behaviors often get a pass in organizations
where their role or individual talent is valued over others'.

Willful blindness to reality can be a culture killer. Failing to
acknowledge actions that create negative impact becomes the
lowest common denominator for the entire organization.
Some of the most frequent examples are allowing verbal or
emotional abuse, a constant violation of values, or breaking
company policy.

For the broader team, it becomes a memorialized symbol of
preferential treatment. Their conclusion is that *they don't matter*,
resulting in passive disengagement. The collateral damage from
not simply DWYSYWD — doing what you said you would do —
is a high price to pay. There's an easy button. Be resolute about
and address what you claim is imperative, and the rest will take
care of itself.

Reflection Pointes

What are you tolerating culturally that deserves to be addressed?

If you hold onto what your culture claims is important, what decision does this lead you to make?

Proactively, what will you do in leading the way for what will and won't be accepted within your team or organization?

How will you stay accountable, even if the person's contribution from a performance perspective is impactful?

Weekly Pointe of Wisdom

You don't have a culture problem. You have a top-level leadership problem. An unhealthy culture is merely a symptom.

At the risk of being polarizing, here's the shocker: Culture is *not* the *primary* issue to focus on in organizations today. To help add to the realization, I'll take this one to the mat. It's about this: Being a leader who lives, breathes, and unwaveringly models the organization's values and guiding principles. *If this exists, culture will take care of itself.*

While we should have our fingers on the pulse of the culture, allocating resources to what addresses the root cause and symptoms of an ailing culture yields the greatest ROI. Invest in the leaders who set the pace for culture.

- Hire leaders who can prove they've demonstrated the values in other organizations and roles, to ensure they're compatible with the demands of the culture.

- Set performance management and accountability measures around values and cultural synchronicity. Promote those who perform in alignment with values.

- Deeply involve and reward those who engage as cultural champions.

Reflection Pointes

In what ways are you best supporting the aspirational culture within your team and company?

As you reflect on your leadership style and most common behaviors, in what one area do you sometimes fall short?

How is this one area misaligned with one or more of your organizational values?

Starting today, how will you course-correct this area?
Who or what can you call on to help you?

Weekly Pointe of Wisdom
*I've regretted some things;
being generous isn't one of them.*

There are seasons in our lives where we don't have as much time or money. We're taking care of children or aging parents, reaching a business, career, or financial milestone, or juggling any number of other life realities that take our energy and resources. However, as we move into a season when time and money are available, we're called to be stewards.

One of my favorite and long-standing clients calls it out correctly, relying on age-old wisdom, "To whom much is given, much is required."*

Opportunities to give might include:

- A fifteen-minute check-in with a friend, family member, or co-worker you know needs a lift in spirit.

- Picking up the grocery or food tab for a family or elderly couple you see at the store or restaurant who appear to be struggling.

- Sending prepared food or groceries to a team member or neighbor who's sick or grieving.

- Passing along a job or business connection.

- Making it a habit to ask, "How can I most help you right now?" after a meeting or brief encounter.

Out of gratitude for what we've been given, generosity can flow.

*Luke 12:48

Reflection Pointes

Based on your current life season, what's the number-one way in which you can be most generous — through your "time, talent, or treasure"?

What giving opportunities or organizations are you most passionate about? How can your generosity shine here the most?

If you picked one easy way to demonstrate daily generosity, what would that look like?

What's your quarterly or annual generosity stretch goal?

Weekly Pointe of Wisdom
*When your desire to fly is greater than
your fear of falling, you just jump.*

My 60th birthday present to myself was a skydiving experience. While I was fearful — of the parachute not opening, landing in the wrong spot, or even possible injury — it didn't stop me from jumping.

Fear and desire are the two primal instincts that motivate all our actions. Most are surprised to learn that these two drivers are not opposites. In reality, they're not that far apart. While fear is connected to a feeling of loss, desire is the offshoot of fear that is hopeful for gain. The fear of not fulfilling this bucket-list item was closely connected to and created the desire to experience the feeling of flying.

The Chinese ideogram for "Danger" is the same as the one for "Opportunity." When you become focused on fulfilling the opportunities that either you create or that are available to you, danger loses its power. You can fly.

Reflection Pointes

What's a goal or item on your wish list within your reach that feels both dangerous and opportunistic?

Why is it important to you to achieve it?

How does your "Why" give you the needed inspiration to tamp down the fear?

What will happen, and how will you feel if you never try it? What opportunities exist if you do?

Weekly Pointe of Wisdom
*The reason you may not understand someone else
is that they're not you.*

If you find yourself saying, "I don't understand why s/he would
do that." or "What could s/he possibly have been thinking?"
then welcome to the world of individualism. Remember that
song we sang in Kindergarten, "There's nobody else in the world
like you, nobody else like you!"? It was actually true, and not just
an early morning music filler. Other people are not you.

According to the Clifton StrengthsFinder™*, there's a universe of
34 Strengths that reside in all of us. Depending on our makeup,
each Strength has a different level of intensity and application.
Our unique blend of these Strengths dictates what we're best at
contributing, how we might overuse or underuse a Strength, as
well as how we might become triggered. Why is this important
to recognize? Because 75% of weaknesses are Strengths being
either overused or underused.

If others don't respond the way you would, it doesn't make
them a bad person. It makes them a different person from you.
Isn't that wonderful?

Reflection Pointes

Who, within your sphere of influence, do you least understand?

How do their actions most commonly collide with yours?

Even if you haven't taken the StrengthsFinder™ Assessment or other tools that might provide deeper information, using your own experiences and insights, what are some actions to take to close this gap?

Choose a path to understand this individual more fully.

- Have a conversation with them about what you most need from each other to be more successful together.

- Take the StrengthsFinder™ Assessment to learn more about your Strengths.

- What additional approach(es) would you like to try?

*For more information on the Clifton StrengthsFinder™, visit www.gallup.com.

Weekly Pointe of Wisdom
*When you operate from a place of intrigue and curiosity,
it's impossible to become angry.*

When someone's behavior surprises or frustrates you, how
do you typically respond? Do you:

- Non-verbally display confusion, frustration, or any
  other fitting emotion?

- Express your feelings verbally?

- Withhold emotion or expression in the moment and remain
  frustrated internally?

In the exploration of a recent Weekly Pointe of Wisdom, we
focused on our differences with others. When we don't know
how to respond or want to respond from a healthy place, the best
approach is through the lens of curiosity and wonderment.

- "I'm curious, what could have caused this behavior?"

- "How might something else completely unrelated be
  prompting their reaction?"

- "How closely or remotely does this resemble what I've seen
  in this individual *consistently* — or is my assessment based
  on something the person has done only *recently?*"

Reflection Pointes

What recent situation have you encountered when you could have used more curiosity instead of leaping into an emotional reaction?

If you took any of the three approaches of intrigue outlined, what difference could it have made?

Think about an upcoming conversation or meeting that could stir up some emotion. Instead of reacting in that moment or passively ignoring it, what proactive measures can you take *now* to prepare yourself for holding a position of curiosity?

In daily conversations, practice taking a "pause for the cause" of curiosity. Wait four seconds before responding. What happens?

Weekly Pointe of Wisdom
*What you say "No" to may be more important
than what you say "Yes" to.*

Many titan business leaders including Sheryl Sandberg, Jeff
Bezos, and Tim Ferris attribute much of their success to their
ability to say "No." Realizing that time is a finite resource, as
previously noted in a Weekly Pointe of Wisdom, they guard their
calendars with the utmost care. This has given them the option to
say "Yes" when it matters most.

The current popular phrase for the tendency to opt in too much
is "FOMO" — the "Fear Of Missing Out." Conversely, the "Joy of
Missing Out," or "JOMO," is representative of the choice
of freedom from opting out of an invitation or request. However
you describe it, the takeaway is evident. If we say "Yes"
to everything, then everything matters. If everything matters,
then nothing matters.

When we start to make choices for our time based on what we've
identified as the one, two, or three most important things in
our world, life becomes simpler and more fulfilling. Our path
becomes acutely clear. We become effective at what creates the
most meaning for us.

Reflection Pointes

What causes you to say "Yes" most often?

When you look at all the items on your calendar over the last month, in retrospect, what could you have said "No" to?

Create a case for saying "No" when it doesn't serve your professional or personal priorities. Is it one of the following? Which one resonates with you and applies to the "No" items above?

- "I want to help. However, it's not the best timing for me. Thanks for understanding."

- "I'm not able to attend due to a conflict. Team member X will attend instead."

- "It feels like the project is moving as expected. Send me the highlights from the meeting."

- Other?

For the next 21 days, say "No" to at least one item each day.

Quarterly
Wisdom Reflection Pointes

What one applied Pointe from the journal has been most meaningful for you during the past quarter?

How has this made you a better leader or person?

What is the story or narrative you can share about this shift with others, so that the impact continues within your team and organization? A potential story outline might look like the following:

- "Here was the situation…"

- "Here's what prompted me to work on it…"

- "Here are the actions I took that mattered…"

- "The positive outcome/s include…"

- "How might a similar approach help you in any of your current situations?"

Additional Reflection Pointes

Weekly Pointe of Wisdom
*The positive power of your leadership brand is
in direct proportion to your authenticity.*

Authenticity is when you're true to yourself and your behaviors, regardless of the pressure you may be under to act otherwise. When heart, soul, and actions are aligned, your authenticity quotient is high. You feel free and energized. Your authentic brand garners respect from others due to the integrity of who you are alongside who you profess to be.

When there's a gap, you create the risk of having an inauthentic brand as a leader. It's confusing for others as they attempt to determine who you really are. Trust is compromised. Engagement and loyalty suffer.

Self-awareness is the birthplace of authenticity. When you unequivocally know who you are and come from a place of wanting to honor your best self, life and work are fulfilling and enjoyable. You don't have to pretend to be anyone else, because who you are is more than enough.

Reflection Pointes

What are the three to five words you believe others would use to describe you?

Ask the people who are closest to you how they would answer the "three to five words" question: How closely do your words align with theirs?

What behaviors do you demonstrate that mirror these words?

Based on these behaviors, what is your authentic leadership brand?

Weekly Pointe of Wisdom

You can train and equip individuals in the desired competencies with success. If the system they are operating is non-supportive or broken, the system will win every tim

Organizations across the globe collectively spend billions of dollars on talent development. Training typically consists of a program or one-time event. Coaching is based on a process. Both of these, along with on-the-job application, can be an answer for elevating associates and leaders. Success is within reach only if there are systems and leaders in place to help integrate the new learning.

What does full support and encouraged immersion look like?

- The areas of development focus align with the scope of the role and needed growth.

- The learning is incorporated into the expectations and goals that are part of the organization's performance management experience.

- A platform for the associates to share what they are learning both in 1:1 meetings and in team settings is provided.

- The new competencies are applied to a current project or part of the company's strategic blueprint.

To earn the highest ROI possible from investing in development, make sure you and your organization are willing to pour in the sweat equity needed to optimize the outcome. Only then will it be the gift that keeps on giving.

Reflection Pointes

How do you and your organization view and respond to development? Is it:

- a box to be checked?

- an investment you're willing to go all-in on supporting internally with the required follow-up?

- a way to performance-manage team members you're not willing or able to develop?

Depending on your answer, what steps do you need to take to ensure that your approach to talent development is hardwired for success?

What changes are needed to allow for full integration of new competencies and learning?

What does the change management mission look like this quarter or in your upcoming strategic planning experience to begin to shift this pattern?

Weekly Pointe of Wisdom

People often say they want the truth about themselves or (situation they are navigating. The amount of honesty they (willing to receive ties to their ability to vulnerably receive i

"Just be honest" is a phrase we've all heard from a willing soul who is seeking feedback. You've likely encountered this from leaders, team members, or even friends who are looking for your input and advice. By returning this pointed request with the following questions, you can guide the other person to uncover the real truth.

- "Based on all you've shared with me, what do you believe to be true? How did you get to this conclusion?"

- "If you asked three other people, how would their interpretation of truth compare?"

- "How does what you are starting to surmise about truth stand up against the organizational values? Using these as a litmus test, what's the truth about this situation?"

This path typically allows truth to emerge without imposing yours. After using this approach, it's likely the person will reach the answer on their own. If they're still not there, then ask, "May I share what I'm hearing based on what you've communicated?"

Reflection Pointes

How does the outlined approach to inquiry compare to how you would normally manage a reality check when asked for it?

Think of a current situation where truth needs to be dealt with or exposed.

How might you use any of the outlined questions to help tease it out? Think about the individual and their typical level of vulnerability. Factor this into your plan.

Start to practice this method in lower-risk situations. What happens? How does the other person respond?

Weekly Pointe of Wisdom

People believe more what they say than what you tell them.
Persuade through involvement.

If you want to influence others, ask them what they think first. As a consultative salesperson early on in my career, this was the underpinning of our sales model. Then, as a training specialist, our team developed others with the maxim, "People don't like to be sold — they like to buy." All these years, this has continued to be a shelf staple.

One of the top challenges you are likely to face as a new or experienced leader is the temptation to *tell* instead of *ask*. A foundational skill as a coaching leader is modeling the way for others to see the advantages of selling through involvement instead of telling. The power of the ask can surface the needed input from others to help create a more compelling case.

The human mind needs to be involved to be engaged. How we perceive is based on our ability to process through our own filters. To use a popularized saying, "Tell me, and I forget. Teach me, and I remember. Involve me, and I learn."

Reflection Pointes

What's your typical MO (modus operandi) when trying to persuade, influence, or change a person's beliefs and behaviors?

In considering a recent example, what approach have you found has the most impact?

As you plan for an upcoming meeting or conversation that requires persuasion, how will you influence through involvement? List your questions below.

Post-meeting, reflect on what worked and what didn't. How will you leverage this experience to influence more effectively moving forward?

Weekly Pointe of Wisdom
*When surfacing an issue requiring discussion,
stay "above the line" for the most productive outcome.*

Choosing to stay "above the line" means you choose the words
that will evoke a more objective, less-emotional response. Asking
"Why did you do X?" or "Who was responsible for Y?" can
negatively trigger others because it can sound accusatory and
pointed. The simple use of "Why" and "Who" tend to question
the approach or the person and suggest blame. These kinds of
words — and the responses they elicit — are "below the line."

The words "What" and "How" feel more open and curious.
The following examples illustrate this.

- "How did we get here?"

- "What could we have done differently?"

- "How can I help or be more supportive?"

- "What one thing can we all commit to do moving
  forward to make sure this doesn't happen again?"

Two simple words like "What" and "How" can make all the
difference in how others experience and connect to both the
problem and the solution.

Reflection Pointes

- When did you use the words "Why" or "Who" and experience defensiveness or disengagement?

- Using this same scenario, what could have happened if you had substituted the words "What" or "How" instead?

- Incorporate the recommended questions into your conversations when you are debriefing a situation and/or providing feedback.

- What positive responses and behaviors do you start to notice?

*Many claim original thought for this concept. While I don't, it's been part of my coaching for more than a decade. It deserves a spot in your Wisdom Toolkit.

Weekly Pointe of Wisdom
*You can either spend your time needlessly trying to convin
someone who doesn't get it or invest a fraction of the time
educating and influencing someone who does.*

If you've seen the movie, *The Pursuit of Happyness*, then you've
witnessed the classic case of flawed transactional selling. Chris
Gardner was a literal "beat the pavement" salesperson who
lugged around a heavy piece of medical equipment trying to
sway physicians to buy his product. While we were all rooting
for his success in overcoming his abysmal circumstances, it was a
no-win approach in persuasion.

Whether it's a prospective client or a team member we're trying
to influence, the principle is the same. Don't ever use up energy
trying to influence someone who isn't motivated to act.

Wait. Isn't this what selling is about — convincing someone to
buy something they don't even know they need? It depends, but
largely, not. *Consultative* selling is about first learning the need
and then educating with facts and a relatable story about how
what you're promoting can close the gap between their current
and desired states.

Facts tell. Stories sell. If they're not inspired to act after you've
demonstrated how their stated and real needs can be met
through facts and supporting stories – they may not be a fit.
The sooner this is accepted, the sooner you can move on to
the person who's ready.

Reflection Pointes

When have you invested too much time and energy trying to convince the wrong person or stakeholder?

What were you choosing not to acknowledge about the person, their situation, or their motivation to be influenced?

We all "sell" daily. What can you change in your approach to make it more effective? Ask more questions? Share pertinent data? Tell a relatable, inspiring story?

When you redirect your efforts toward the right approach and the right people, what happens?

Weekly Pointe of Wisdom
Not everyone can be mentored, coached, or helped.

In carrying the torch of leadership and developing your team's talent, it's easy to overlook this reality. You can apply best practice training, coaching, and other techniques, yet not make the needed progress. It's fair to ask, "Is it me? "Have I thrown all the available resources at their performance?" Calling on an earlier Pointe of Wisdom, you can ask yourself, "Is the system supporting them?" All of these are questions that must be wrestled with before you make the call on continuing.

If you examine all three of these areas, and the role and expectations have been made clear, then it's time for resolve. The comment I hear most often in these situations is, "I wish I'd made the hard decision sooner." Hindsight provides the gift of seeing all the investment in a person who wasn't hardwired for success. Delaying the inevitable never makes it easier.

The common adage "Hire slow, fire fast" should be applied early and often as a measure to both avoid hiring or working with the wrong person and remedying it quickly when it happens. Holding on too long delays you in finding the right person, and it prevents them from finding the right fit. Appropriate "letting go" is a win/win.

Reflection Pointes

Who or what are you holding on to that's delaying a needed decision? What's stopping you from deciding and moving forward?

Given the nature of the obstacle you're acknowledging, what's one way to begin to navigate around or through it? Who can you call on to help you?

What's your belief regarding the following statement? "If they could have met expectations by now, they would have." How does it apply in this situation?

Write down your action plan for addressing this situation. What is your timeline for each action item?

Weekly Pointe of Wisdom

*If you want your team to excel at creativity
and innovation, you have to make it safe to fail.*

In working with rapid-growth companies, the recognition of what's at risk invariably shows up front and center. Unconsciously, based on the higher-than-ever stakes, bullish desire can convert into fear. The result is leaders falling into preserve and protect mode rather than continuing the same pace of growth. Derisking shows up as abandoning innovative ideas or not accepting any failures, even though the lesson learned could lead to an even greater future ROI.

If you want to continue growth, failure must not only be safe, but celebrated. Through trial and error, failure creates a more familiar path for what not to do. Singularity in approach and lack of optionality will stifle even the most creative team members. Make space for creativity and failure.

Navigating innovation and creativity at any organizational stage lies in an iterative, milestone-based strategy. This makes failures smaller and the opportunity to pivot more possible. Encouraging a "Let's be creative in getting there first but fail fast if it doesn't work" mentality makes all the difference in an organization's ability to perpetuate growth and avoid stagnation.

Reflection Pointes

Reflect over the past few weeks. What messages might you have unknowingly given or actions have you taken that closed down possibilities-based thinking?

With a current initiative or strategic mission, how can you lead in a way that opens up more space as well as reward for creative and innovative thinking?

If fear of failure is the one variable preventing you from accepting failure, how can you make it more incremental and less detrimental?

How does the long-term impact of this approach offset any shorter-term losses?

Weekly Pointe of Wisdom
*The path to freedom begins with knowing what
you can control and what you can't.*

Personal energy consumption and regeneration often drive our ability to be at our best. When you expend too much energy on what's outside your locus of control, it taps into your reserve for what could be channeled more effectively and efficiently to what's inside of it. Where do you want to be most impactful?

When you delineate between these two positions — internal or external control — it frees up your focus to drive excellence in what matters most. We're often reminded to keep perspective through the "lens-of-time" rule. Will this matter six months from now? One month from now?

Keeping a healthy perspective on the flurry around you will prevent giving over too much power to those areas that you don't control and that don't matter in the bigger scheme. If you focus on showing up at your best and brightest place with an awareness of what you're truly able to impact, it reduces unnecessary drama and distraction. As leaders with important missions, we can all sign up for this. In the coming weeks, make it so.

Reflection Pointes

Make a list of the energy you are devoting to both the things you can and can't control. What does this reveal?

Examine the list of things you're acknowledging that are outside your locus of control.

What about each of them pulls you in? How can you break this habit?

If you make a pact with yourself to redirect your energy to those things within your control, how can you start today?

Weekly Pointe of Wisdom

*Before you burn political capital, make sure you
have a fire extinguisher or safe exit nearby.*

It's a wise leader who is able to pause and ask, "Is this a battle
worth choosing and fighting?" A loss of impulse control, either
habitually or momentarily, can put a chink in the brand armor
or, even worse, take you to the point of no return in regaining
what you've worked so hard to build. What are you willing to
proverbially fall on your sword for?

Warren Buffett reminded us, "It takes twenty years to build a
reputation, and five minutes to destroy it." Keeping this front
and center, you can more mindfully manage your response
to your areas of passion to make sure the investment of
disagreement or time spent is purposeful. Is the thing you want
to champion a time-bound belief or a typical trigger?

Yes, leadership is sometimes about taking a stand no one else
is willing to take. If leadership were easy, as the saying goes,
everyone could do it. However, examining your depth of
conviction around any well-intended crusade is worthy
of a deep dive.

Reflection Pointes

Choose a project or initiative currently under consideration for implementation or one that is being rolled out that you have strong conviction around. Where do you stand emotionally and objectively?

If it's one that you feel you need to take a stand for or against, what do you need to consider from a political-capital standpoint? What are you willing to risk? Is the reward worth it?

Based on earlier Weekly Wisdom work that focused on influencing through involvement, what is a path of persuasiveness you can take in this situation? What can you do or ask to both involve and influence?

Who are your co-champions?

Weekly Pointe of Wisdom
EQ is your winning edge in leadership.

In recent years, research consistently reveals that emotional quotient eats intellectual quotient for breakfast, lunch, and dinner. Of course, intellectual horsepower is imperative as one price of entry. However, all else being equal, EQ separates the top-shelf leader from the leader who struggles consistently with crucial components in the emotional responses to work and life.

Is it time to examine your EQ edge? These components of the EQ wheel* form the foundation of your result. Building upon each other, the goal is to keep them in balance.

- Self-Perception™ — how you regard yourself, self-actualize to your potential, and form awareness of your emotions.

- Self-Expression™ — how you express your emotions and assert yourself; the level of independence or dependence you use.

- Interpersonal™ — the mutual satisfaction of your relationships, your use of empathy, as well as the social responsibility you exhibit to those both close to you and in your larger ecosystem.

- Decision-Making™ — your ability to solve problems objectively, reality-test against data, and use appropriate impulse control in deciding.

- Stress Management™ — the flexibility, stress tolerance, and optimism applied day-to-day.

Reflection Pointes

In your new awareness or review of these components, which one is most out of balance for you?

If you start with Self-Perception, what are some actions you can take to become more aware of self?

Acknowledging that journaling elevates self-awareness, what or who else is available to help?

Looking at your current position scope and what's ahead for you, use the EQ components as a checklist for monitoring your application of EQ in the most critical situations. What happens?

Weekly Pointe of Wisdom

Your intention to be proactive affects everything you do, including who you become as a leader.

Show me a proactive leader, and I'll show you a leader who's strategic and thoughtful. They're in control of their business and role. In fact, they manage all aspects of their life with greater ease. As a result, their happiness quotient is higher, and their stress is lower. This journal is filled with many compelling cases built on maneuvering time and talent. The best-in-class leaders aren't perfect, yet they skillfully harness many of these steps.

On the other hand, we all hold anecdotal examples of leaders who fail to take control because they don't choose control. They don't choose control because they don't believe it's an option. Or they may choose the path of least resistance. This mindset and approach unfortunately lead to missed opportunities, misery, and occasionally even a victim mindset.

Seeing the possibility of being in charge is the first step, believing the probability of it is the second, and making it happen is the third step. Proactivity is possible for you and every leader who claims it. You, and only you, are in charge of you.

Reflection Pointes

In what areas of your life and work are you most reactive
and least intentional?

In what one or two areas can you start to be more proactive by
taking back and reclaiming control?

What boundaries do you need to create to make this a reality?

Write "I'm in control" on a blank card. Post it on your mirror so you
see it each morning. Say this mantra to yourself each time you move
into the next segment of your daily schedule. What changes do you
start to see in yourself?

Weekly Pointe of Wisdom

In a world crowded with consumers, be a creator.

A connection on LinkedIn publicly shared her decision to leave her position. With this announcement, she was seeking input on how to fill the gap she was taking before pursuing her next role. She posed the question, "What should I do in my time off?" A flood of responses filled the screen. "Here are the books you should read"… followed by a list. "There's a great Netflix documentary series on….," another chimed in. A well-intentioned list of advice continued to stack up.

In taking a notice of the recommendations, not one of them suggested, "Pursue a long-held passion," "Start something new," or "Reflect on where you've been and write blogs or a book." The theme was clear—it was all about consumption.

We have a myriad of options for how to use open space in both small and large windows. At the end of our time, what will truly matter is what we choose to create that improves someone's life or makes the world a better place. If our obsession is consumption, the opportunity will be foregone.

Does your internal tape tell you that you're not creative? Then practice. Try something. Build something. Just start. Your breakthrough may be just one, two, or three steps away from significant, game-changing impact for yourself and others.

Reflection Pointes

How many hours do you spend weekly consuming information? As you do a quick audit of screen time and your calendar, what do you notice about where your margin time goes?

What have you created or contributed to, that you're most proud of? How did you arrange time and space to get there?

Moving forward, how can you rearrange your world to allow for more creation and less consumption?

How can this one change of becoming a creator make a lasting impact on your legacy and how you're remembered?

Quarterly
Wisdom Reflection Pointes

What one applied Pointe from the journal has been the most meaningful for you during the past quarter?

How has this made you a better leader or person?

What is the story or narrative you can share about this shift with others, so that the impact continues within your team and organization? A potential story outline might look like the following:

- "Here was the situation…"

- "Here's what prompted me to work on it…"

- "Here are the actions I took that mattered…"

- "The positive outcome/s include…"

- "How might a similar approach help you in any of your current situations?"

Additional Reflection Pointes

Yearly
Wisdom Reflection Pointes

What have you learned about yourself as a leader?

Which Pointes of Wisdom had the most meaning?

What are the specific pieces of sage wisdom you're carrying away from the applications suggested in this journaling experience?

Which areas will you continue to work on in order to deepen your wisdom?

Who are the sages, and what are the resources that will guide you?

"The first step to becoming wise is to continue to look for wisdom."
Proverbs 4:7

Additional Reflection Pointes

Praise for The Way to Wisdom:
A Leader's Weekly Guide

"In the twenty years I have known Teresa, she has consistently provided business executives with innovative tools to take leadership to the next level. By adopting Teresa's leading-edge approach in, *The Way to Wisdom*, leaders can utilize this effective pathway to drive themselves and their organizations forward to achieve desired results."

Drew White – CFO, Tesseract Ventures

"*The Way to Wisdom* is a great guide for those who want to increase in wisdom and leadership skills in their various vocations and circles of influence. The lessons in this year-long journal truly are ageless and well-proven in life. The accompanying questions will provide the leader with the space and time that we all need to live life well. I heartily endorse this book!"

Kevin Rauckman - Garmin Retired CFO

"Teresa leads us on a thought-provoking journey with simple, yet powerful questions that prompt us to reflect, explore, and navigate with intention. If you are ready to live and lead from a place of wisdom and lasting impact, you will love *The Way to Wisdom*."

Danna Demos – Director, Division Advisor Development Executive, Merrill Lynch Wealth Management

"*The Way to Wisdom* is structured with weekly leadership wisdom followed by reflection pointes that support you in determining how to put that wisdom into action for you personally. It creates an opportunity for you to take new ideas and not just simply catalogue them, but to live them. I highly recommend it."

Marty Bicknell - CEO, Mariner Wealth Advisors

"Wisdom from Teresa G. Carey (whom I wish to dub The Coach 'LExtraordinaire') can be found in her new book *The Way to Wisdom*. It's a concise 52-week adventure into your future self. The book it is easy to implement and not burdensome with all of the over obligations I have in my life. It gets to the core of what you purpose! Bravo, Teresa!"

David C. Seitter – Attorney and Partner, Spencer Fane LLP; Author, "Quiet Plans – Exciting Results: 47 Trusted Secrets to Big Business Success; Podcast Host – "Show Me the Way"

"*The Way to Wisdom: A Leader's Weekly Guide* has been a valuable resource for our team. We've integrated it into our talent development process. The experience of holding weekly wisdom circles each week has provided thoughtful introspection and sharing of effective ideas among the group."

Amanda Burnett – Director, Human Resources, 12-48 Holdings

"This book is such a gem! The journaling provides a great way for leaders to reflect and gain wisdom from the author along the way. It makes a great gift for those in your professional network."

Emily Blue - Co-Founder of Hue Partners

"da Vinci said, 'Wisdom is the daughter of experience' and Teresa Carey has plenty of both. Having worked with the author, she is easily one of the top 5 professionals I have enjoyed learning from over my 40+ year corporate career. Her book is a comprehensive weekly guide that will develop your leadership wisdom. It provides a holistic approach to cultivating inner wisdom. I love the journal prompts as the end of each section."

Jeff Pelaccio - Marketing Executive;
Podcast Host – "The Corporate Couch"

"Teresa has profoundly shaped my career and leadership style, extending her impact to my teams, peers, and broader network. Her wisdom, often shared through thought-provoking questions, has been my guiding light through work challenges, growth opportunities, and my development as a leader. Teresa shares that wisdom broadly through her fantastic book *The Way to Wisdom-A Leader's Weekly Guide*. I recommend this book to leaders in any stage of their career."

Jen Ashlock - Director of Marketing, Weitz Investment Management

"*The Way to Wisdom: A Leader's Weekly Guide*, has been a game-changer for my team and me. We spend 15-20 minutes each week diving into leadership lessons from the book, discussing thought-provoking questions, and applying the insights to our daily lives. This process has not only challenged me as a leader but has also helped us strengthen our team's camaraderie and connection."

Zack Bailey - Director of Human Resources and EEO Officer,
Superior Bowen

ABOUT THE AUTHOR

Teresa Carey's mission is to liberate the
greatness within others. Through her
intention and curiosity, she taps strengths
and inner wisdom to enhance professional
performance. Working with pre-rapid and
rapid growth organizations, Teresa serves
as a trusted coaching partner to top C-Suite
executives and leaders. She founded her
strategy and coaching firm more than three
decades ago.

Teresa G. Carey

Today, Teresa's clients at PeformancePointe, Inc.
describe her as compassionate, strategic, and insightful.

The Way to Wisdom illuminates the experience and insight
in Teresa's work with leaders. While the world of business
has changed dramatically over the past 30 years, the truths
in this work are immutable. She is the author of a previous
book entitled *The Attractive Trap: Freeing Yourself from an
Unhealthy Relationship*.

Teresa is passionate about family, food, and fitness –
competing as a triathlete and runner. She is a devoted
mother and grandmother, as well as an avid reader
and writer.